Original title:
Diving into the Unknown

Copyright © 2025 Creative Arts Management OÜ
All rights reserved.

Author: Lucas Harrington
ISBN HARDBACK: 978-1-80587-398-3
ISBN PAPERBACK: 978-1-80587-868-1

Beyond the Veil of Certainty

In the land of what ifs, we twirl and we spin,
With each step we take, where will we begin?
A map drawn in crayons, directions unclear,
We might find a treasure or just a lost deer.

A leap off the couch, my cat joins the cheer,
Chasing shadows of dreams, and hoping for beer.
Mysteries waiting, we giggle and shout,
Is it fortune we're seeking or just the way out?

Journeys into the Obscure

Through the fog of confusion, we wander and roam,
With laughter our compass, we make every place home.
Tangled in thoughts like spaghetti in sauce,
Each twist is a mystery, with nary a loss.

We chase after echoes, like children at play,
Pretending to know what we don't, anyway.
With each silly question, the answers all jest,
We find joy in chaos, it's truly the best.

Footprints in the Dark

In shadows we shuffle, unsure of our feet,
With giggles and gasps, each corner we greet.
A flashlight's a friend, though it blinks like a star,
Illuminating secrets that seem just bizarre.

A creature darts by, but it's just a shoe sock,
We laugh at ourselves, our own little flock.
Each step brings surprise, a dance in the fright,
Footprints in darkness, a comical sight.

Where Angels Fear to Tread

We wander where wisdom would rather not go,
With giggles as armor, and spirits aglow.
A sign says 'Caution', but we wave it away,
What could possibly happen? Oh, come on, let's play!

In places where logic is tossed like a ball,
We trip over reason, and still have a call.
With humor our beacon, we laugh 'neath the dread,
In places where even the angels get fed.

Echoes of the Abyss

I twirled with a fish, thought I'd learned a new dance,
But it swam away quickly, quite fast in advance.
I waved to a crab, he stared back in dread,
Guess I'll stick to the shore, or swim home instead.

A mermaid appeared, with a tail made of cheese,
She offered me snacks as I sank to my knees.
With bubbles and laughter, we shared quite a feast,
Then she swam off, my cheese dreams had ceased.

Silent Waters

With goggles and flippers, I made quite a splash,
The fish all looked on, and then started to dash.
I waved with a smile, then got tangled in seaweed,
Turns out, underwater, I'm not what they need.

I thought I was graceful, like a swan on the jet,
But a crab found my toe and it's not done yet.
With arms flailing free, flippers flying about,
The ocean's a laugh when you're filled up with doubt.

Hidden Worlds

I found a snug nook, thought I'd stay for a chat,
But the octopus giggled, and now I'm the brat.
He tossed me a shell with a wink and a curl,
Next thing, I know, I'm off to a whirl.

I joined in a dance with a fish in a tie,
He said it was formal, I just had to try.
With bubbles and wiggles, we spun 'round the reef,
Then I tripped on a rock, and laughed through my grief.

Through the Misty Abyss

Where jellyfish float, and the dolphins are wild,
I spotted a treasure, was it fate or a child?
With a wink and a giggle, I dove in with glee,
Turns out it was seaweed, not gold, oh, me!

A whale sang a tune, oh, what a great sound,
But then he mistook me for plankton—oh wow!
With laughter and bubbles, we shared quite a jest,
The ocean's a stage, and I'm just the guest.

Boundless Horizons Await

I hopped on a wave, thought I'd surf like a pro,
But the board had its plans—it just wanted to go!
I skidded and splashed, made a scene oh so grand,
And ended up dancing with fish and with sand.

So here's to the plunge, here's to fortune and fun,
With friends who are fish, every day's just begun.
Go sing with the seals, take a leap, take a chance,
In the water, each moment can lead to a dance.

Mapping the Unfathomable

In a sea of wobbly charts,
With squiggly lines and funny parts,
I set out with my rubber duck,
To find where all the fish had struck.

Compass spinning, I took a guess,
To find the treasure, no more, no less,
But all I found was a jellybean,
A sticky gift from the ocean's scene.

My map was drawn by a playful dog,
Barking orders as thick as fog,
Yet every step was filled with cheer,
Who knew the ocean held such beer?

In this great chase, I danced and slipped,
While sandcastles stood, worried and tipped,
My journey seems a silly jest,
Yet laughter echoes through each quest.

Soaring Intrepidly

I leaped from clouds like a feathered clown,
With mismatched socks, I spun around,
My parachute was a picnic sheet,
As I tumbled down, I chanced to greet.

Fish in top hats cheered me on,
While squirrels juggled at twilight's dawn,
A flight of fancy, a whimsical race,
Up in the air, my socks lost their place.

I landed soft on a pile of hay,
With giggles echoing, come what may,
But my lunch flew by, a sandwich on a spree,
It waved goodbye, as happy as can be.

The sky's my stage, with stars that wink,
In a twist of fate, I learned to think,
Soaring madly, a sight so bold,
Adventure awaits in stories untold.

Unfolding Mysteries

Beneath a blanket of playful stars,
I hunt for answers in dusty jars,
Old riddles whisper in curious tones,
But as I ponder, my cat just groans.

The moonlit path is filled with jest,
Each turn I take, a funny quest,
A talking frog claims it knows it all,
But left me tripping, just to sprawl.

Amidst the shadows, I take a peek,
Mysteries tumble, then go to speak,
I found a sock, a treasure disguised,
With stories of adventures that left me surprised.

Each clue I find leads to a grin,
As socks and frogs dance cheek to chin,
In this game of silliness galore,
The mysteries make me laugh more and more.

The Beauty of the Unseen

In the gardens where the shadows play,
Napping flowers bloom bright as day,
I sought for colors hidden from sight,
And stumbled on a worm in a fright.

A sunbeam whispered secrets low,
As I twirled in a hula-hoop show,
The beauty around made me twinkle and sway,
Invisible giggles were here to stay.

The groundskeeper's dog wore a crown,
Chasing his tail, spinning round and round,
With each twirl, I found a new cheer,
In all the quirks that drew me near.

Beneath the laughter of petals sweet,
Life's hidden wonders are meant to greet,
So I laughed with the unseen sounds of glee,
Finding joy in all that wasn't just me.

Venturing Off the Map

I packed my snacks with a hint of dread,
The compass spins, my map's a spread.
With humor tucked inside my pack,
I stumble forth, no clear-cut track.

A llama waves as I step right out,
It grins so wide, there's little doubt.
I trip on rocks, the groans ensue,
But laughter bubbles; it's a wild crew.

A signpost reads, 'This way or that!'
I choose the path with a silly hat.
A squirrel grins as it takes a bite,
Of an apple bright in the morning light.

But what do I find as I wander lost?
A treasure map with frosting glossed.
Turns out the quest was cake all along,
Who knew the path could be so wrong?

Embracing the Unfathomable

In a sea of socks, I lost my mind,
I turned each shade, I hoped to find.
The ocean waves called out with glee,
Let's jump, they said, just you and me.

A whale in shades gave a wink my way,
'Take the plunge!' it seemed to say.
I slipped on seaweed, belly flop,
Bubbles burst, and those giggles never stop.

Around the reef, I twirled and spun,
A crab in a bow tie joined the fun.
With crabby jokes, it danced with flair,
While jellyfish tangled in my hair.

I swam with fish who'd dance and prance,
Each flip and flop a whacky chance.
With every stroke, I laughed out loud,
Turns out the deep's just one big crowd!

The Call of the Abyss

A echo calls from the depths below,
'Take a leap! You'll never know!'
With fins like flippers, I jump right in,
Splashdown laughter, let the fun begin.

What lurks beneath? A dolphin's grin,
Winks and flirts, dance begins.
I twist and swirl in a madcap show,
Lost in the current, in a flowy flow.

A giant octopus, arms spread wide,
Grabs my goggles, joins the ride.
With eight-legged flips and a splashing flair,
We plot mischief 'neath the ocean's stare.

As bubbles rise, I start to see,
The motivation's fee, just joy and glee.
A pirate ship wrecked with jokes to tell,
We laugh and swim, oh so well!

Unexpected Shores

I set sail on a rubber duck,
With dreams afloat and a touch of luck.
The tides took me, oh so spry,
Past jellybeans and donut pie.

A whale's a bear with a tie and top hat,
It chuckles, 'Grab a snack, how about that?'
I dined on cupcakes, the ocean's fair,
With salt on the rim and sweet in the air.

As I rolled upon the laughing waves,
A crew of crabs played musical knaves.
Drumming shells to a jazzy tune,
Who knew the ocean? A grand festoon!

At last I found an upside-down shore,
With sand that's sweet and sweets galore.
I laughed and played 'til the sun went low,
Unexpected shores make the heart grow!

Plunge into Mystery

With a splash, I take the leap,
Hoping to find secrets deep.
Fish doing yoga, what a sight,
They giggle as I sink from flight.

Bubble troubles fill the air,
Where did I leave my extra pair?
Mermaids laugh and wave hello,
"Is that your foot? Or just a shadow?"

I find a treasure, or so I think,
Turns out it's just an old pink sink.
Nautical maps lead me astray,
Cartographers surely love to play.

So here I float in feathery bliss,
Perhaps I should have practiced this.
Fins and flippers, what a design,
Next time, I'll stick to the shallow line.

Embracing the Void

I wobble, I tumble, I welcome the fall,
Is this adventure or just a brawl?
Jellyfish glow like disco balls,
Dancing beneath as my bravery stalls.

A sea turtle winks, oh what a tease,
Should I follow or take it with ease?
Coral reefs whisper, "Step right in!"
But I'm tangled up—oh wait, is that a fin?

I churn in circles, bubbles my friends,
Laughing at thoughts of rules and bends.
"Is this not like the movies?" I say,
Fish roll their eyes, "Not in this ballet!"

So here I swirl, in giddy delight,
Who knew the depths brought such a fright?
Maybe I'll float on this happy ride,
Or play it cool, with fish as my guide.

Shadows of the Unexplored

Peering out past the water's edge,
Can I leap off? Should I hedge?
A crab just winked, it's quite suspenseful,
"Join us!" they cheer, making life simple.

I squint my eyes and take a chance,
But an octopus pulls off my pants!
"Fashion forward! Don't you see?"
I float yet wonder, was that a spree?

Underneath, the seaweed sways,
Singing songs in watery ways.
Pirate ghosts wave their old flags high,
Saying, "Don't be shy, just give it a try!"

So here I tread on this slippery ground,
Life's a comedy, where fun is found.
Each shadow's a giggle, a chuckle, a cheer,
I survive the mischief, without any fear!

The Call of Depths

What's this ruckus down below?
A chorus of laughs, a clownfish show!
I snorkel down to see the fun,
End up tangled—oh, what a run!

A dolphin grins, "You've lost your shoe!"
I shrug and say, "Well, what's new?"
Eels sneak up with giggles and jests,
In this underwater carnival, I'm their guest.

"Join the parade!" the sea stars chime,
What a strange twist on the passage of time!
I cartwheel through, feeling quite bold,
Though the fish behind me look rather cold.

I pop to the surface, breathless and wild,
Making memories with my inner child.
The unknown calls, like a wiggly spree,
Next time with snacks—just add some sea tea!

Chasing the Invisible

Lost in a fog, can't see my shoe,
A fish just sneezed, how rude, who knew?
The bubbles rise, like giggles in air,
I'm flapping around, without a care.

Wobbly fins, my dance is a mess,
Giggling seahorses, they just digress.
I trip on a shell, oh what a blunder,
The ocean's a stage, and I'm the thunder.

With laughter in waves, I float and I spin,
Tickled by currents that pull at my grin.
A crab makes a dash, I cheer for his race,
Life under the waves is a whimsical place.

I'll chase every shadow, swim with a smile,
The ocean's my playground, let's stay for a while.
In search of the sillies in depths oh so blue,
Who knows what I'll find? A clownfish that's new?

Treading on Unfamiliar Shores

With toes in the sand, I dare to explore,
A jellyfish wiggles, I can't take it more.
In flip-flops I stumble, a tumble, a fall,
The tide waves and whispers, 'Give it your all!'

The crabs wave their claws, they're judging my style,
I slip on a seaweed, land in a pile.
A dolphin just giggles, a splash from behind,
I'm soaked to my bones, feel the love of the kind.

Shells crack and they laugh, as I trip and I spin,
Each step is a journey, an adventure within.
With every new wave, I just let out a squeal,
Oh, treading on shores can be quite a big deal!

The sun's setting low, with colors on fire,
So many new pals, it never gets dire.
The beach is a realm, where mishaps are gold,
In awkwardness, thrills, let the stories be told.

Secrets of the Deep Blue

In waters so dark, with secrets to keep,
I met a strange fish, it felt like a leap.
It winked, it whirled, and said with a grin,
'What's life without laughter? Let's jump right in!'

A treasure chest waits, but it's buried in sand,
A mermaid pops up, with a seashell in hand.
She giggles and twirls, in the moonlight we play,
The octopus joins, in a fanciful sway.

With jellyfish flying, glowing like stars,
We dance with the waves and go chase some guitars.
A clam tells a joke, but it's crusty and old,
Yet laughter will echo, a treasure untold!

In the depths where the secrets spin 'round and 'round,
We swim through the sillies, with laughter profound.
Dive in with a splash, there's no need to be blue,
Life's a grand party in oceans so true!

Embracing the Charcoal Horizon

The sun dips away, casting shadows so thick,
I stumble on sand with my dancing sea tick.
In twilight's embrace, I tumble and roll,
The waves chuckle softly, it's good for the soul.

I chase after gulls, not a plan in my head,
They giggle above me, with feathers instead.
I slip on a kelp, oh what a delight,
Embarking on antics that last through the night.

With stars popping out like a flickering cheer,
I'm launching myself into dreams without fear.
The whispers of tides have stories to tell,
Of mischief and magic, oh can I rebel?

The charcoal horizon, canvas so vast,
Paints laughter and joy, oh this day is a blast.
So come on, dear friend, let's jump just as we may,
In embrace of the night, let's indulge in the play!

Tales from the Abyss

Bubbles rise as I take a plunge,
Flippers flapping like a wild grunge.
Fish give me side-eyes, do they suspect?
I'm just seeing if I can do a perfect wreck.

My snorkel's stuck, I look like a clown,
Gurgling giggles while I float upside down.
A squid waves hello with a wiggly jig,
Oops! There goes my snack! It spins like a pig.

Seaweed wraps tightly, like a sporty scarf,
While jellyfish join in for a little laugh.
I dance with the crabs, what a silly sight,
When they snap their claws, I take flight!

As I finally emerge, what a ridiculous scene,
Salt stuck in my hair, face green from the green.
Friends can't stop laughing, "You should wear a tie!"
Next time I'll leave the deep sea to the fishy guy.

Ominous Horizons

I squint at the waves, oh what a fright,
Is that a shark? Or a seal in the night?
My brave heart whispers, "What could go wrong?"
I plummet forth singing a silly song!

An octopus grins with eight arms to spare,
My goggles fog up; I can't see anywhere.
He offers me a ride on a turtle's back,
But I'm pretty sure turtles can go off track.

I spot a treasure chest, am I the bold?
Turns out it's just kelp, a humorously old.
The fish roll their eyes, do they know my plight?
"Just stick to the sun, dear, don't give us a fright!"

When I swim back, legs like jelly and weak,
Everyone asks if I took a peak.
I smile and nod, keeping secrets well-kept,
Like how I just sang, and how the fish wept!

The Veil of the Unknown

With goggles on tight, I ease in with flair,
Splashing like a toddler, I know they all stare.
The depths call my name, but wait, what's that sound?
A dolphin's rude giggle? I'm lost and I'm drowned!

Beneath the blue ripples, oh what a sight,
A turtle's slow dance, such grace and delight.
But hang on a sec, is that a fish brawl?
They vie for my snacks, they're having a ball!

What's this tiny critter joyfully peeking?
Is that a pufferfish, or a friend just seeking?
I swear they're all laughing, oh what a show,
As I learn how to swim with my flippers aglow.

Finally back up, I'm gasping for air,
My friends can't stop chuckling, they won't even share.
Next time I'll buy floaties, not take a risk,
And skip all the fish drama, it's getting too brisk!

The Allure of Hidden Waters

Heed the call of the sea, what could go wrong?
With fins like a mermaid, I'll play all day long.
But beneath the blue, I find what I sought,
A crab with a top hat! This is quite the plot.

"Welcome, dear swimmer, to our fancy ball!
Where sea cucumbers dance and plankton enthrall.
But watch for the jelly, they tickle and squeeze,
A cheeky distraction that's sure to tease!"

Amidst the corals, the treasures do hide,
A rubber duck floats, a whimsical ride.
I join in the fun, twirling round with the tide,
As dolphins applaud, I feel full of pride!

Then back on the shore, I slip on some chips,
With seaweed on my face and a laugh on my lips.
The ocean's allure, it's quirky and wild,
Next time I'll return, like a giggling child!

In Search of Forgotten Tides

Once I leaped where fish retreat,
Chasing shadows with my feet.
A dolphin tried to steal my hat,
I yelled, "Hey buddy, that's not for you!"

With goggles fogged, I swam amiss,
Got tangled up in seaweed bliss.
The octopus waved a friendly hand,
And I replied, "This wasn't planned!"

I met a crab with fashion flair,
Wearing shells without a care.
We danced a jig beneath the swell,
Till I tripped on some fishy gel.

Now I laugh at tales I've spun,
Of all the sea things I have done.
So if you hear a splash and yell,
Just know it's me, and all is well!

The Depths of Curiosity

With a snorkel and a big ol' grin,
I plunged right where the fun begins.
A treasure map led me astray,
To find a shoe instead of pay!

A turtle winked, as if to say,
"You'll find more here than gold today!"
I chased a jelly, oh what a sight,
It jiggled and danced; oh what a fright!

I tried to ride a dolphin's back,
But landed smack in some seaweed crack.
Laughter bubbled in ocean blue,
As fish giggled at me too!

Oh happy day, my quest complete,
With salty hair and sandy feet.
I'll tell my friends of things I've seen.
While they all wonder, what does it mean?

Echoes from the Unfathomable

In the depths, I thought I'd hear,
The secrets whispered, crystal clear.
What I found was a shrimp parade,
They were dancing; oh, what a charade!

Anemones waved, a colorful show,
I tried to join, but moved too slow.
A seahorse laughed; I gave a frown,
And flipped my fin to turn around.

Bubbles formed like tiny cheers,
As fish clapped with their fins, it appears.
I couldn't help but giggle too,
At the ruckus all around the blue.

Every echo held a friendly tune,
While I wished to find hidden boon.
But if the sea just wants to play,
I'll stick around, come what may!

Beneath the Ripple

What lies beneath the shimmering wave?
Surprises lurk, but must I be brave?
A starfish waved a sleepy hand,
I stifled a laugh at his sandy band.

A clam yelled out, "Stop by for tea!"
I said, "I'm busy, but thanks, you see!"
With curious eyes, I pressed along,
To a fishy choir singing a song.

The anglerfish gave a scary grin,
But turned out he was just joking, akin!
As bubbles floated, I cracked a smile,
Who knew the sea could be so worthwhile?

With my trusty fins, I twist and twirl,
Among the wonders of the underworld.
Each ripple tells a laughter-filled tale,
Of absurd journeys that'll never pale!

Embracing Chaos

In a whirlpool of socks, I lost my shoes,
My cat gave me a look, I can't refuse.
The kitchen's a circus, the fridge is a zoo,
Who knew breakfast could turn into stew?

Chaos is laughter, with sprinkles of fright,
When I try to bake, I just start a fight.
Eggs fly like pigeons, the flour's like snow,
In this silly madness, I'm ready to go!

Turn up the music, dance on the floor,
Spaghetti's for dinner, or maybe a chore?
Lost in my laughter, with friends by my side,
Embracing this chaos, let's take in the ride!

With a wig and some googles, I'll surely take flight,
The world is my playground, everything's right.
In this zany riddle, I choose to play fair,
Life's just a circus, but hey, I don't care!

Awakening the Brave Heart

Woke up one morning, the mirror went boom,
I greeted my hair like it lived in a tomb.
Sword made of shampoo and shield from a brush,
Today's adventure has started with a rush!

I donned my cape, which is really a sheet,
Set out for the garden, where dragons retreat.
With my trusty sidekick, a squirrel named Pete,
We fought off the weeds; now that's quite a feat!

Each step a tango, with flowers as foes,
To conquer the backyard, where magic still grows.
My heart whispers loud, "Let's go chase the sun,"
But first, let's find snacks, that's part of the fun!

Through bushes and brambles, we find candy dreams,
A treasure of laughter, bursting at the seams.
Awakening bravery, in mismatched shoes,
The world is our stage, with nothing to lose!

A Journey Beyond Borders

Packed my suitcase with socks and a hat,
Tossed in a fish, and oh! Look at that!
A map made of chocolate, a guide full of cheese,
I'm off on a journey; I'll go if you please!

Last seen at the zoo, my suitcase went wild,
It chased down a monkey, heartwarmingly styled.
Together we ventured, a duo of thrill,
We danced with the penguins and gave zebras a chill!

Crossing new borders, with giggles and bliss,
I captured the moments; I wouldn't want to miss.
A passport made of candy, it's all in good cheer,
Let's book the next flight, adventure's right here!

Just hold on tight, the ride's full of glee,
With the circus around us, come take a seat.
A journey awaits, past borders we'll roam,
In this world made of laughter, we are never alone!

The Strangeness of Solitude

In my quiet corner, the sock puppet speaks,
He shares all the tales of his wild two weeks.
The goldfish gave pointers, the chair gave advice,
Creating a party, and for free, it's quite nice!

Echoes of giggles bounce off the wall,
With nobody here, I still feel so tall.
I danced the cha-cha with my muffin on plate,
In this strange solitude, I'm always first rate!

The curtains are closing, the mirrors applaud,
Who knew being solo would feel so avant-garde?
With a bubblegum crown, and pajamas that shine,
I reign in my kingdom, it's all by design!

So if you feel lonely, don't fear being quirk,
Invite in the silliness, it's all in the work.
Embrace every moment, let your spirit ignite,
In this strange solitude, everything's bright!

Into the Abyss

With goggles on, I take a leap,
My belly flops, a splash so deep.
The fish all laugh, they point and stare,
While I'm just searching for my spare pair.

Bubbles float like silly balloons,
I swear I saw a mermaid's tunes.
But nope, it's just a plastic bag,
I chase it down but then I lag.

My flippers flip, a wild parade,
I trip on seaweed, what a cascade!
The sea's my stage, I'm quite the clown,
A flip, a flop, then I drown.

I rise back up with a grin so wide,
In this wacky wave, I'll take my ride.
So here's to the depths, so full of cheer,
With every splash, I've got nothing to fear.

The Uncharted Depths

With a snorkel stuck on my nose so bright,
I venture forth, oh what a sight!
Tropical fish in a dance, they sway,
I join their groove in a goofy ballet.

My map's upside down, lost as can be,
Turns out the treasure was just my keys.
I wave to a crab, he gives me a scowl,
While I'm thinking, "Is that how I prowl?"

Algae hugs my leg, what a surprise,
I think it's a friend who wants to rise.
But no, it's just muck, refusing to leave,
I try to shake it, "You're a real weave!"

Under the waves, it's quite a jest,
Every bubble's a giggle, what a fest!
So if you're lost, don't shed a tear,
Just laugh with the sea, it's all sincere.

Beneath the Surface

I slipped on a rock, it's slippery slick,
But beneath the waves, I still make my pick.
A turtle zooms past, giving me a grin,
"Join the race, buddy! Let's see who'll win!"

I flail my arms, like a crazy bird,
The fish just chuckle, but they've not heard,
I'm searching for treasure, or maybe a snack,
But all I see is an old shoe rack.

A school of fish flashes by like a train,
I wonder if they'll share their gain.
They circle around, it's a wild retreat,
"Guess we're stuck here, it's a fishy meet!"

From depths of despair to laughter galore,
This oceanic dance, I simply adore.
With each twist and turn, it's plain to see,
The ocean's a comedy, come swim with me!

Whispers of the Unseen

Under the waves, I hear them sing,
A chorus of crustaceans doing their thing.
I join in the song, a startling surprise,
But they all swim away, rolling their eyes.

The deep blue holds secrets, or so I'm told,
Like the snack I lost, how very bold.
I hope it's just hiding, but a seal gives chase,
"Hey buddy, mind your personal space!"

I flip over rocks, see what's beneath,
It's a treasure trove, but I'm befriending a wreath.
"A plant, a friend!" I shout with glee,
As it wraps 'round my foot, "Oh, woe is me!"

With giggles and splashes, I dance with delight,
In this watery realm, everything's light.
So here's to the whispers that make me grin,
In the heart of the ocean, let the fun begin!

Embracing the Enigma

With socks on my hands, I start the quest,
Mismatched shoes seem to pass the test.
A map made of cheese, I can't find my way,
Laughing at puzzles that lead me astray.

The compass spins round, it's got a mind,
Each turn I take, more lost, I find.
But hey, it's a journey, not a race,
In this carnival ride, I'm finding my place.

With giggles and gasps, I wade through the odd,
An umbrella for rain, a fish in the fog.
Who knew confusion could spark so much glee?
Join me in chaos, come dance with the silly me.

The end of the road? Oh, what a surprise,
A circus of wonders, a feast for the eyes.
So grab your quirks, let's see what's in store,
Embracing the weird, there's always more!

The Lighthouse of Mystery

In the beam of the light, a cat wears a crown,
Sailing on donuts, spinning around.
A parrot in shades squawks, strictly for laughs,
Charting a course with slapstick gaffes.

Behind every door, a joke's tucked away,
I tripped on a riddle, all I could say.
Each wave that crashes, a giggle unleashed,\nMystery swirls like whipped cream on a feast.

The neighbors are squirrels with spectacles fine,
Discussing the weather over glasses of wine.
They argue with owls, both wise and absurd,
In this wacky retreat, the odd is preferred.

So come to the shore where the quirks convene,
With laughter resounding, it's a sight unforeseen.
Where shadows perform and the moon sings a tune,
We'll dance with the goofy under a starry monsoon!

Echoes from the Void

A vacuum of giggles, what's that I hear?
Is it a ghost popping corn, oh dear!
With echoes of laughter that bounce off the walls,
I'm joined by the dreams in my panda-print stalls.

I sipped from a strange cup, it fizzed and it whirred,
A hiccup of nonsense escaped every word.
The shadows are casting some witty old puns,
As I chase the sound of imaginary runs.

In a world made of jelly, confusion feels sweet,
Jumping in puddles that wobble on feet.
I'll skip through the unknown, don't mind if I fail,
The more that I tumble, the brighter the trail.

Each echo a giggle, a riddle, a tease,
Whispering secrets on flamboyant leaves.
Here's where nonsense and joy intertwine,
Echoes embracing this fun, divine!

Journey Through the Unfamiliar

With shades on my forehead, I'm off on a spree,
Llamas in tutus are waiting for me.
I packed up my backpack with snacks for the road,
A treasure of jellybeans, my secret code.

Each turn that I take opens doors to delight,
A bridge made of marshmallows, oh, what a sight!
I tickle the cloud that drifts cheerful and round,
In this jolly adventure, giggles abound.

The path might be silly, but I'm feeling bold,
Chasing after shadows, a story unfolds.
A penguin on roller skates leads the parade,
And laughter erupts in this cavalcade.

So join in the fun, leave your worries behind,
Add a dash of whimsy, let joy be your guide.
Through the quirky and weird, we'll dance with the day,
In this labor of laughter, let's twirl and sway!

Shadows of the Depths

Bubbles float while fish do dance,
A jellyfish winks, oh what a chance!
Shrimp throw parties, crabs go wild,
Here in the ocean, I feel like a child.

Seaweed whispers secrets and pranks,
Octopus paints with all of its flanks.
A sudden splash, oh what's that sound?
Just my lunch, lost and found!

Down where the sun loses track of time,
Mermaids laugh, oh what a crime!
But I forgot 'til now, to smile with glee,
I wore my flip-flops, not fins, you see!

As I chase a rogue dolphin that's free,
I stumble on coral, oh look at me!
The depths are a circus, every turn a jest,
In this grand wet show, I'm merely a guest.

A Plunge of Faith

I took a leap, not knowing the task,
What's lurking below? Why must I ask?
With shorts and a sigh, off the edge I tumbled,
Into a realm where sanity crumbled.

Crabs are critiquing my splash and my dive,
Fish roll their eyes, yet they seem so alive.
A pirate ship sinks, but there's no gold,
Just a rubber ducky, is this what I'm told?

With every wave, my worries just fade,
A seaweed wig, oh look, I've got it made!
The deeper I go, the funnier it gets,
But I should've packed snacks, the ocean forgets.

So here I float in laughter and cheer,
For in this grand scheme, there's nothing to fear.
With fishy companions, I dance through the blue,
Life's just a party; come join in, it's true!

Veils of the Unseen

What's behind that curtain of foam?
A dancing squid? Or somewhere to roam?
The waves are giggling, the tide takes a bow,
I've lost my shoe—where did that go now?

A treasure chest lies, but full of old socks,
The sea's fashion sense is quite paradox!
I'm chased by a fish that's sporting a wig,
Its laughter erupts, it's doing a jig.

With every swirl of the salty ballet,
I ponder how weird this world is today.
There's murky mischief hiding all around,
For every swirl, a new joke gets found.

So come take a peek, it's a world full of fun,
Where squids wear glasses and fish join in on the run.
The veils of the depths are silly and bright,
Let's frolic forever, till day turns to night.

The Call of the Uncharted

What's splashing about in this wobbly sea?
A mermaid's karaoke, singing just for me!
The tides are laughing, a pearl that went 'pop!'
No map in hand, but I won't let it stop!

The sea turtle chuckles, "You're lost, my friend!"
As I paddle in circles, a wobbly trend.
Shells throw a rave; they're all having fun,
While starfish giggle, I'm under the sun.

The treasure I seek? It's nowhere in sight,
But the fish are all laughing—it feels so right!
My naiveté fuels this aquatic parade,
With laughter and silliness, I'm happily swayed.

So here I wander, no fear of misstep,
With laughter and joy, I take every prep.
In these waters so strange, I'm never alone,
No maps needed here; I've found my way home!

Tracing the Unknown Path

With every step, the map is wrong,
I wear my compass like a thong.
The trees are laughing, birds call out,
'Where are you headed? What's this about?'

As mud pulls at my shoes like glue,
I swim through leaves of vibrant hue.
Oh look, a rock that looks like cheese!
I swear, it wiggles when I tease!

A squirrel flashes its tiny grin,
'Lost again? You'll never win!'
But what's this noise? A bubbling brook,
I must explore! But what's that nook?

With every turn, I find a laugh,
A dancing weed, a jumping calf.
I might be lost, but what a show,
Tracing paths where wild things grow!

The Siren's Call

From rocks arise a haunting tune,
It seems to pull me, like a balloon.
In sparkling waves, I see a face,
'Join me here!', whispers from the place.

I swear it's serious – no time to flee,
But wait, is that a crab? It's winking at me!
The seashells giggle with salty zest,
I might just stay, they seem the best!

The mermaids swim with glittering hair,
'Come have a sip of our ocean air!'
But down below, I see a shoe,
It's definitely not from me or you!

Who brought this trash to my sweet shore?
Tangled nets and bottles galore!
Siren, dear, you've lost your charm,
I'm off now! Your sea's too warm!

Encounters in the Dark

In the shadows, things start to creep,
Something giggles as I lose sleep.
I trip on air, my heart goes boom,
A raccoon winks from a hidden room.

A whisper floats on drafty air,
'Come play with us! We do declare!'
But cobwebs spin around my sock,
Are those the hands of a little clock?

I point my flashlight, oh what fun,
A band of snakes just start to run!
A squeaky voice says, 'Don't be shy!'
I'm really trying, but - oh my, oh my!

Fluffy shadows come out to play,
With each flicker, they sway and sway.
In these mysterious, silly nights,
My fears take flight in laughter's heights!

The Depths of Discovery

Zooming down in a bubble car,
Past fish that look like outlandish stars.
A silly octopus waves a paw,
'Thank goodness you came! We need more law!'

He hands me a map of candy reefs,
'Watch out for sharks, they're big and beef!'
With jellybean corals all aglow,
I can't wait to see where we'll go!

A cow that swims with goggles bright,
'You found our secret! What a sight!'
Lollipops float where sea turtles glide,
I can't wait to go for a ride!

Down here, every turn is pure delight,
Where gummy bears dance through the night.
With each silly twist in this underwater quest,
The depths of fun are simply the best!

The Unmapped Journey

With compass spinning in dismay,
I jumped on in without a say.
A map? Oh please, who needs those tools,
Just follow the giggles and the swimming fools.

The water's cold but the laughs are warm,
I flounder 'round, a fishy charm.
A seaweed wig makes quite the crown,
Who thought exploring could be this clown?

A squawk from a gull, a splash from a seal,
Every blunder turns into a reel.
Sandy socks and soggy shoes,
I'm rated five stars in oceanic ooze!

With each wrong turn, I learn to glide,
In this chaos, I take such pride.
To twist and tumble, all's good fun,
Adventure starts when plans come undone!

Tides of Transformation

The tide rolls in, I'm feeling bold,
A splash of color in waters cold.
With flip-flops on, I'm quite the sight,
Cartwheeling sideways, what a delight!

The fish all giggle at my grand show,
As I trip over rocks and over my toe.
With seaweed braids and a crustacean friend,
It's a party on waves till the daylight ends!

I met a crab who wore a hat,
Gave me a wink, "Hey, how about that?"
Together we danced, and it was grand,
Who knew the ocean could be so unplanned?

But as the moon pulls at my soul,
I decide to let the sea take control.
With a whirl and a twirl, I lose my sense,
In this wet mischief, I find my immense!

Beneath the Surface

Bubbles rise like giggles in the air,
I ponder if there's treasure down there.
With snorkel gear and a rubber duck,
My serious face? Oh, I've run out of luck!

A dolphin darts past, giving a wink,
While I'm stuck here, trying to think.
Where's the gold? I only find guppies,
Perhaps my quest ends with silly puppies!

A pirate's dream? More like a snooze,
Finding fish socks is what I choose.
With every flip, my hopes start to sway,
Oh well, at least it's a funny display!

As the sea pulls me deeper in,
I think of life and just start to grin.
For every stumble, every little miss,
Riding the waves is pure bliss!

Shadows of the Unknown

In the twilight where shadows play,
I leap right in, come what may!
With a floatie shaped like a giant cat,
I'm ready to swim, first off, how 'bout that?

The murky depths hold secrets untold,
Yet I spot a clam, it's doing the fold.
With pearls for eyes and laughter galore,
Even sea creatures can't take it anymore!

A hermit crab in a tuxedo coat,
Said, "Have a seat, let's rock this boat!"
We twirled and spun, in fishy delight,
Who knew shadows could party all night?

Yet as dawn breaks, I float back to shore,
Leaving behind the depths I adore.
With ocean magic and giggling tides,
The unknown holds fun where adventure resides!

Voices of the Deep

In the depths where creatures prance,
Silly fish in a tango dance,
Octopus plays a game of peek,
As we wonder, 'What do you seek?'

With gurgled laughs and bubbles blown,
A whale sings tales of the unknown,
A clownfish cracks a joke or two,
While sea cucumbers play it cool.

A sea horse looking quite perplexed,
Can't find his shoes; he feels annexed,
Coral reefs whisper secret rhymes,
As starfish count their endless times.

So here we float, what a delight,
With goofy pals in colored light,
Exploring depths, who knows what's near?
Just keep your snacks, oh, always here!

Rolling into the Unfamiliar

We hop aboard our bouncy raft,
The ocean waves give quite a laugh,
With every roll, we squeal and slide,
What a wild, wacky ocean ride!

A jellyfish floats by with flair,
In its tentacles, we lose our hair,
The pelicans watch, they take their bets,
On who will fall in first, no regrets!

A crab says, 'Hey, not so fast!'
As we zip by, the boat's a blast,
While dolphins giggle, the seas swirl,
We stumble and trip in aquatic twirl.

So raise your glass to salt and wave,
In unfamiliar, we misbehave,
The ocean's pulse, with humor sings,
Rolling into what laughter brings!

Chasing Distant Dreams

Beneath the waves where weird dreams dwell,
A fish named Fred knows all too well,
He chased a star a bit too far,
Now he's stuck in seaweed, quite bizarre!

The turtles laugh, 'What's your big plan?'
As Fred works hard, his tail like a fan,
The anglerfish lights up the way,
While we cackle 'Is that night or day?'

With a wink from the old octopus sage,
He says, 'This sea is but a stage!'
So we dance along, not feeling blue,
In dreams that swim, we'll laugh anew.

Who knew the sea had jokes to tell?
Each creature's quirks cast a funny spell,
So let's keep chasing what's out of reach,
With giggles tucked in our beachy speech!

The Surge of Unchartable Waters

In waters where the maps are blank,
We paddle on, a wild prank,
Here's wishing on a floating log,
That navigating won't feel like a slog!

A dolphin zips, then does a flip,
While we hang tight and start to slip,
Clinging on to each other tight,
As fish hop by, laughing in delight!

A seagull squawks, 'You're lost, my friends,'
But we just wave, the fun never ends,
With every wave, a joke is spun,
In uncharted seas, we're never done!

So let the surge lead us astray,
Where laughter's found in the fray,
With every splash and gentle sway,
We'll find our joy in the silly play!

Whispers from the Deep

Bubbles rise, a silly dance,
Fish in hats take a glance.
Octopuses wear ties so neat,
Waving hello, oh what a treat!

Sandy spirals, a gnome appears,
Sipping seaweed, quenching fears.
Mermaids laugh, a jolly crew,
Who knew the sea was this much fun too?

Underneath a yawning whale,
Jellyfish glow, telling a tale.
Crabs are cracking jokes, quite sly,
While dolphins jump up to the sky!

Treasures lay in a rubber chest,
Where sea turtles take a rest.
With every splash and silly jest,
Who knew the deep could be the best?

Fearless Descent

Down we go, swish and sway,
Finding fish like child's play.
Goggles on and funny fins,
Ready for our watery wins!

In the depths, where mermaids hide,
Flipping past an octopus wide.
With every twist, a laugh we share,
Even seaweed's got some flair!

Bubbles pop, tickle our toes,
A crab comments, 'Look at those!'
With giggles echoing through the blue,
We swim and play, the fearless crew!

Fortune's glow in sunken ships,
Where pirates hide their silly quips.
With treasures bright and laughter loud,
In the depths, so fun, so proud!

Secrets of the Waters

Underneath the wavy crest,
Fish are wearing their best vest.
Seashells whisper secrets sweet,
While starfish wear their best front seat!

Giant squids do the cha-cha,
While clownfish chuckle, ha-ha-ha!
Seahorses dance with whimsical flair,
Jellyfish float like they don't care!

What lies beneath, oh what a show,
Treasure maps that lead to... Whoa!
Crazy critters with antics strange,
In the ocean, life's a range!

From the shore, we laugh and cheer,
In this world, there's none to fear.
With every splash, the fun's revealed,
Secrets in the deep are unsealed!

Abandoning the Shore

Leave behind the sandy beach,
As we float, so fun to reach.
Silly dolphins in a line,
Bouncing high, oh how divine!

Fish flip-flop like they've lost the plot,
Starfish giggle, 'What a spot!'
Crabs serving shrimp on a plate,
In this sea, we celebrate!

Waves are laughing, come and see,
An anchovy's got a degree!
Adventurers free from boring lore,
Sailing forward, can't ignore!

In the tides, we find our way,
With every splash, we sway and play.
Life's a joke beneath the sun,
In the sea, we're all just having fun!

Whirlpools of Wonder

In a pool of ideas, I spin and swirl,
Like socks in a dryer, in a fun, wild whirl.
What comes out next? A t-shirt or shoe?
Best grab a snack, or maybe two!

With rubber ducks floating, I laugh and scream,
The water's a canvas, a place for a dream.
A splash of confetti, and I'm swept away,
In this whirlpool of wonders, I choose to play!

The bubbles rise up, they tickle my nose,
Like bubbles from soda, how quickly they go!
If I hold my breath, I'm sure to float high,
But hey, who needs air? Just reach for the sky!

So here in this vortex, I'll twirl and glide,
In the pool of absurdity, come take a ride!
A flip, a twist; oh what a sight,
The whirlpools of wonder keep my day bright!

Unknown Currents

What's lurking below in the wavy expanse?
A fish with a top hat? Perhaps a dance!
Each stroke forward brings giggles and grins,
Just hope that the seaweed won't tickle my shins!

With goggles on tight, I quest through the blue,
Invisible wonders seem eager to view.
A jellyfish winks, and I shout out in glee,
"Excuse me, dear jelly, can you swim with me?"

In whirlpools of mischief, I do a quick spin,
While seahorses giggle, 'Let the fun begin!'
A kraken or two, maybe oddball sea mice,
With friends like these, who needs to think twice?

Each twist of the tide is a laugh to behold,
So I'll stream with the currents, let the tales unfold!
In this zany adventure, we dance and we play,
For what's lurking below is just a splashy buffet!

Resilience in the Unforeseen

Bouncing through chaos, I trip and I fall,
A tumble, a giggle, do I see it all?
With each little stumble, I gather my might,
Turning fumbles to fortune, oh what a sight!

A pelican's swoop, a surprise dive to eat,
I land on a surfboard, with toothpaste for feet!
It's slippery business, but laughter's the key,
I swirl with the waves, feeling wild and free!

When the seabed surprises, with creatures so strange,
I wiggle and wobble, adapting to change.
From octopus dances, to crabs in a race,
In this wacky adventure, I find my own space.

So here's to resilience, and laughter that grows,
In currents against currents, where anything goes.
With joy as my lifeboat, I'll surf through the night,
For in the unforeseen, I find my true light!

The Edge of the Known

At the brink of the water, I scratch my sweet chin,
Thinking of mermaids, and eating a fin!
With toes dipped in madness, shall I take a leap?
Or just jump in and find a treasure to keep?

What hides in the depths? A riddle or jest?
Maybe an octopus, wearing a vest!
With laughter as my buoy, I float to explore,
Finding a fish with a top hat, oh what a score!

The splash of the unexpected tickles my toes,
With seashells that giggle, and starfish that pose.
I gather my courage, I splish and I splash,
At the edge of the known, it's a raucous bash!

So come join my circus, it's wild and it's real,
With jelly-filled laughter and a squishy appeal.
With waves as my canvas, the ocean my throne,
At the edge of the known, I finally feel home!

The Edge of the Unfamiliar

Wobbly feet on the brink of the strange,
I peek over the ledge, my thoughts rearrange.
The fish are all laughing, I swear they can talk,
As I ponder my fate, on this slippery rock.

The clouds seem to giggle, the moon starts to wink,
With one dizzy spin, I begin to rethink.
Do I jump for a splash or just stay in my dreams?
Oh, the water looks cozy, or so it mistakenly seems!

A splash so loud, I create quite a scene,
Did I just find Neptune, or is that just a bean?
My hair's now a fountain, my clothes stuck to me,
Next time I'll wear floaties—or maybe a tea!

The waves start to chuckle as I flail in this plunge,
Why's there a seagull saying, "Take the big lunge"?
In this whirlpool of laughter, I learn to just flow,
Maybe exploring the odd isn't bad after all!

Beneath the Quiet Surface

Bubbles twist and twirl, like dancers on air,
I plummet below with an unlikely flair.
The seaweed does jiggle, my fins do a dance,
As I look for things I can't quite give a glance.

The fish give me side-eyes, what gives them such pride?
Am I the new guest at their underwater tide?
I wave a hello, they just swarm and retreat,
Clearly, I'm not one for their fancy meet and greet!

A clam tries to gossip, but can't quite unhinge,
"Oh dear! I won't ask! That could cause quite a cringe!"
As I sip on the salt with a straw made of reeds,
I ponder the wisdom in their oceanic creeds.

Yet laughter erupts as a crab grabs my toe,
"Just your average pincher, so let's not take it slow!"
With sea urchins chuckling and jellyfish jive,
I realize the weird is what keeps us alive!

Venturing into the Gloom

In shadows so thick, where the creatures reside,
My heart does a dance like it's on a slide.
A toadfish just winked, what a curious sight,
Is he friend or a foe, or a mix of both fright?

The glow of the lanternfish flickers and shines,
A disco of sorts, beneath tangled pines.
What's lurking above, or, is that just my fear?
The bubble of silence, it bubbles up beer!

A giant and grumpy old squid gives a glare,
I wave like a madman; he throws back the stare.
"Who ordered the soup? Served with a side dish!"
I shrug and respond, "Oh, I'd rather not fish!"

With giggles and whirlpools, adventure unfurls,
I'm tucked in the depths of this wild, wacky world.
In gloom there's a glow, as odd as it seems,
Every twist wraps a tale—so vivid in dreams!

A Leap Beyond Reason

What's that lurks in the distance, a bubble or squawk?
With gusto I leap, like a bird on a rock.
Does logic still matter when splashes abound?
In this curious chaos, do I drown or rebound?

I'm soaring like seagulls, or maybe just flop,
As I hope for some laughter, not just a big drop.
With fins that are flailing, I tackle the tide,
Who knew that absurdity is the best place to hide?

A dolphin-gang hijinks, they twist and they twine,
Jostling my bumbles, making fun of my spine.
"Come dance with us, human! We flip, we twirl!"
To this wild wave party, I give it a whirl!

As I navigate waves with a giggle and swish,
I'm just a small fish in this surrealist dish.
In this frothy collage, where convention takes flight,
The leap was the best—oh what a delight!

The Allure of Shadows

In corners dark, where whispers creep,
A dance of shadows, secrets keep.
I stumble forth, with broom in hand,
Beware the dust bunnies, oh so grand!

They giggle low, they roll and play,
I trip and fall, they steal my way.
I chase them 'round with little fright,
In playful games, we share the night.

A sock appears, a shoe goes miss,
A sock that smells of a fishy bliss.
I laugh aloud, this game's absurd,
These shadows dance, oh haven't you heard?

From dusk to dawn, we spin and twirl,
With every twist, my stomach curls.
In silly jig, oh what a show,
The shadows' charm—their allure glows!

Quest of the Boundless Sea

A ship I built from cardboard dreams,
With laughter loud, my mission beams.
I set my sails on the kitchen floor,
With waves of soup—what's there in store?

The goldfish shrieks, 'You can't go far!'
I wink and say, 'Just watch me star!'
With jellyfish jelly in my tea,
I'm the captain of this madcap spree!

The parrot's squawk, my only mate,
With every squabble, we share a plate.
The ocean swirls, it's one fine mess,
A caper of snacks, oh what duress!

Adventure calls, my heart's aglow,
Through liquid dreams, we steal the show.
A treasure map made of crumbs and cheese,
In every bite, exploits to seize!

Into the Abyss

What lies beneath the couch so deep?
A world of relics where lost socks weep.
I take my plunge with a giggle loud,
To find the treasures the dust has bowed.

Old popcorn kernels, a shoe from last June,
A sandwich warped by the light of the moon.
I laugh so hard, the neighbors stare,
As I bumble forth, with crumbs to spare!

A dust bunny kingdom—rulers of fluff,
They chuckle at me, I've had enough!
'You think you're brave?' they tease and say,
It's only dust here, come out and play!

A clump of fur, a banana peel,
This journey's worth it, what a surreal!
I rise with glory, conquering grime,
Oh the victories found in the depths of time!

Beyond the Horizon

I set my eyes on a cake so wide,
With frosting waves, I must abide.
Across the table, a vast dessert sea,
Adventure awaits, it beckons me!

With forks like sails, I chart my course,
A chocolate tide, oh the mighty force!
The jellybeans dance, laughing in cheer,
As I brave this feast without fear.

Frosting storms and sprinkles bright,
Each bite a treasure, pure delight.
I dive headfirst with a spoon so grand,
This voyage of flavor is truly planned!

With every chew, a tale unfolds,
A saga sweet, as life beholds.
So come join me, let laughter reign,
Beyond the horizon, there's joy to gain!

Reflections in the Abyss

With a splash and a giggle, I take the leap,
Splashing water on friends, reactions so deep.
Fins flapping wildly, up goes my cap,
Bubbles around me, what a silly trap!

A fish with a grin gives me a wink,
I ponder my choice while starting to sink.
Noodles and goggles, it's quite a sight,
Is that my old shoe, coming back for a bite?

The echoes of laughter, they float all around,
As I mimic a seal, flopping down with a sound.
Glancing at shadows, they dance with delight,
Who knew swimming could be such a fright?

The unknown calls softly, with giggles and splashes,
Each flip and a turn, through funny little crashes.
A treasure chest glimmers, I wonder what's in,
Pathway of clowns, oh, where to begin!

From Familiar to Foreign

I took my first step on a board so wide,
Underwater worlds that I can't quite abide.
Goggles on tight, I peer through the glass,
Is that a sea cucumber? Oh, what a rascal!

Crabs on a mission, with pincers so bold,
Sneak past my feet, oh they're daring and old.
As I wave at a starfish, it just gives a stare,
Am I the weird one? Do they even care?

Curious turtles, they swim by so slow,
With goofy little grins, oh, how do they know?
They nod as if saying, "Just follow the flow,"
But I trip on the coral and let out a "Whoa!"

Gasps turn to giggles, my friends share a look,
As I tumble on sand like a bumbling crook.
From comfort to chaos, it's totally clear,
Exploring the wild takes a little more cheer!

Pulsing Beneath

What's that stirring? A tickle? A tease?
A jellyfish party, oh please, oh please!
The squishy glow beckons, I think I'll go near,
Will they all dance with me or just disappear?

Beneath the surface, a wiggling swirl,
I'm a wild little fish in this bizarre whirl.
Hands flapping about, I'm part of the crew,
Giggling at bubbles that gather like dew.

A mermaid appears, with pearls in her hair,
"Come join our jam!" she says, without a care.
Together we twirl, just a medley of fun,
In this absurd waltz under rays of the sun.

The rhythm gets wilder, a cerulean beat,
With clownfish and laughter and no chance of defeat.
As time slips away in this whimsical dance,
I wonder if I'll ever get back to my pants!

Heartbeats of the Unknown

A flip and a splash, I swim with a grin,
Echoes of laughter are where I begin.
Each heartbeat a rhythm, each kick a new dive,
Incredibly silly, I feel so alive!

Exploring the depths, I trip on my fin,
What now is this? More fish trying to win!
They dart to and fro, like a joyful parade,
I join in their antics, I hope I'm not played!

Seaweed tickles my toes, a giggle escapes,
With friends by my side, there's no escapes.
Uncharted waters are less scary than thought,
Just where are we going? A new world we sought!

In the heart of the splash, it's laughter that's shared,
With creatures around us, I'm hardly prepared.
But my joy knows no bounds in this vast ocean fun,
Life's an adventure, let's see how it's done!

The Unfamiliar Frontier

With a leap and a giggle, off we go,
Into places where the wild weeds grow.
We'll trip over rocks and dance with bees,
In a land where the mushrooms sing with ease.

The map is a doodle of squiggly lines,
Leading us to where the sun brightly shines.
We'll find cozy caves, or maybe a shoe,
A giant left behind, oh what a view!

Puddles will splash with a big, loud 'plop',
Here in the land where the funny folks hop.
We'll catch a few clouds, and wear them as hats,
Laughing at squirrels that chatter like brats!

So grab your snacks and your wibbly wand,
To the frontier of fun, let's gleefully bond.
With each silly step, let out a cheer,
This place is delightful, oh dear, oh dear!

In Search of Hidden Truths

In the cupboard of secrets, we search for clues,
Among the old socks and forgotten shoes.
With a magnifying glass and silly grins,
We hunt for treasures, let the laughter begin!

The cat winks knowingly, oh what a tease,
As we rummage through drawers with urgent ease.
What's this? A rubber duck wearing a crown?
Royalty found, let's all gather round!

A map drawn in crayon, like a pirate's quest,
Pointing to snacks hidden deep in the chest.
We'll follow the trail of jellybeans bright,
In search of the truths hiding out of sight!

Each corner we turn, there's giggles galore,
Hidden truths hiding behind every door.
It's not just the snacks that we cheerfully seek,
But the joy in the journey, unique and antique!

The Compass of Wonder

My compass spins wildly, no North in sight,
As we wander through wonders both day and night.
With each twirl and whirl, we set sail on air,
With laughter our anchor, we float without care.

Guided by giggles, we follow the fun,
Over hilltops of candy, beneath setting sun.
We'll toast to the bumbles and tumble and spin,
Every twist holding secrets we hope to unpin.

What lies beyond? Is it rainbow, or pies?
A field of balloons? Or perhaps a surprise?
Let's chart our own course, with whimsy and flair,
As the compass of wonder spins tales in the air.

With giggling hearts and dreams spun so wide,
We trust in the silly, come what may bide.
Through thickets of laughter and breezes of cheer,
We'll toast to our journeys, both far and near!

Wandering into the Mist

In the misty terrain where the giggles grow,
We'll find silly creatures who dance to and fro.
With a hop and a skip, we'll blend in the haze,
Playing hide-and-seek in a foggy maze.

The trees are sneezing with branches so long,
As we twirl through the whispers of their playful song.
Clouds tickle our heads as we laugh and we sway,
In this whimsical fog, we'll frolic all day!

The shadows are silly, they wiggle and wave,
As we trick them with jokes in the mist, oh so brave.
With each twisty turn, surprises await,
Beneath laughter's embrace, we'll dance with fate.

So come take my hand, let's dance in the mist,
With each giggle and grin, there's adventure, insist!
In a world full of wonder that pops and it swirls,
We'll cherish this joy, as our laughter unfurls!

www.ingramcontent.com/pod-product-compliance
Lightning Source LLC
Chambersburg PA
CBHW070319120526
44590CB00017B/2736